Made in the USA
Columbia, SC
30 July 2021

42644363R00057